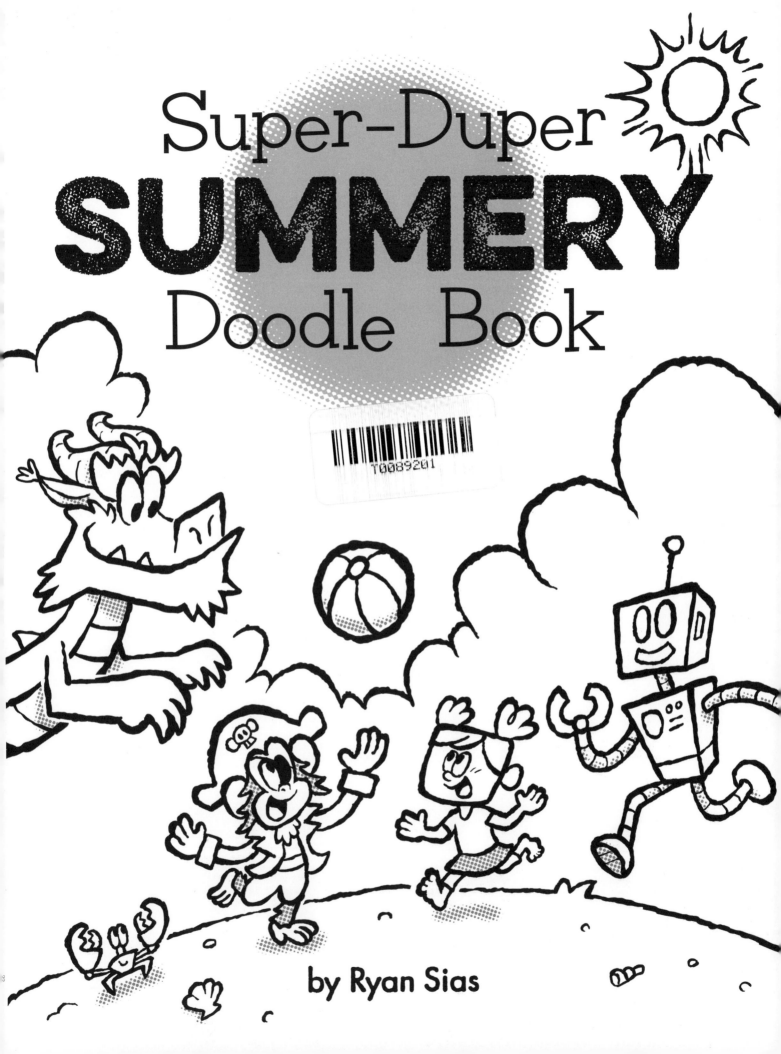

To my parents,

who allowed me to draw all the time.

Text and illustrations copyright © 2018 by Ryan Sias

hmhco.com

The text of this book is set in Graham.
The display type was set in Plumbsky and Eveleth Dot.

ISBN: 978-1-328-81017-5

Manufactured in China
SCP 10 9 8 7 6 5 4 3 2 1
4500697498

Ahoy! It is I, Monkey Pirate Doodler! Argh! I love to draw! Let's start by drawing palm trees.

Now draw LOTS of palm trees on the island!

BONUS! Draw bananas in the trees. Did you know pirates love bananas?

Psst . . . I've hidden 29 suns in this book. Can you find and color them all? Oh! And don't forget to decorate with the stickers in the back of this book!

3

Monkey Pirate

Draw your own.

Draw a Giant Sandcastle!

Give Monkey Pirate
silly swim shorts.

What buried treasures does
Monkey Pirate find in the sand?

What does Monkey Pirate do with the treasure he finds? Write a story.

megaphone
toothpaste
banana
ring
skateboard
sandal
paint-brush
lollipop
rainbow

9

Carla the Crab

Draw your own.

······· BONUS! **How to Draw Shells** ··········

Draw your own.

What does Carla find inside the seashell?

Draw lots of seashells
to fill up the bucket!

Oh no! A storm is coming!
Draw a huge wave crashing on the shore.

Carla finds a message in a bottle.
What does the message say?
Who is it from? Write a story!

Find and Color the Hidden Items

flashlight apple sailboat duck

horseshoe fish heart crown snake

Give Toby Turtle an awesome tropical shirt.

Draw grass skirts on Toby and Tara
so they can hula dance!

Tara Turtle loves her hat made of fruit!
Can you draw it?

HINT! Be sure to include Monkey Pirate's favorite fruit!

Story Starter

Oh no! The volcano is erupting.
What do Toby and Tara do?

Draw your own.

Draw an awesome truck
for Ice Cream Dog.

Find and Color the Hidden Items

23

Story Starter

Describe what happens when
Ice Cream Dog discovers that all of
his ice cream has melted!

  Color all the different flavors melted together.

The sun is too hot.
Draw a beach umbrella
for the sunbather.

Louis is really thirsty.
Draw a twisty straw
for his lemonade.

26

BONUS!
Give the drink a tiny umbrella.

Draw silly sunglasses on everyone.

Story Starter

The seagulls are hungry.
Tell a story about what happens when
Clark eats crackers on the beach.

Find and Color the Hidden Items

broom

mailbox

watermelon

carrot

bacon

Popsicle

mushroom

dolphin

Roller-Skating Rhino

Draw your own.

Draw another
Roller-Skating Rhino
on the boardwalk.

Rhino is looking in a candy shop.
Draw all your favorite candy
in the window.

Creston the Cat loves merry-go-rounds.
Draw an unusual animal for him to ride.

BONUS! Make Owen the Octopus's seahorse a crazy color.

Creston the Cat

Draw your own.

Draw the expressions on everyone's faces as they ride the roller coaster.

BONUS! Draw a silly cat in the empty seat.

Creston is dizzy!
He's headed to the cotton candy
machine. What happens next?

Draw cat fireworks!

Packard Pig

Draw your own.

·········· BONUS! How to Draw Pies ··········

Draw your own.

Draw Packard Pig's friends at the table.

HINT! Draw lots of pies, too!

How many pies can Packard fit in his mouth?

HINT! Make them different flavors.

Packard won first prize in the contest but got pie all over his face. Draw his messy face.

Packard ate the most pies. Draw his prize.

BONUS! Draw how the other pigs feel.

Story Starter

Describe what happens when Monkey Pirate throws a pie at Packard.

Draw your own.

Owen Octopus is playing
Toss the Ring. Draw an octopus
friend to play with him.

.... **BONUS!** **How to Draw Ducks** ....

HINT! Draw more ducks in the pool.

Owen won!
How does he feel?
How does his friend feel?
Draw their expressions.

Draw the prize Owen picks
after winning Toss the Ring.

rocket
surfboard
lock
bowl
bowling pin
carrot
cherries
orange

48

Mr. Robot is going on a trip. What should he pack?

49

Mr. Robot

Different Robot Heads

Draw your own.

Mr. Robot and the family are on a road trip.
Can you draw them?

Mr. Robot is taking a picture with his family
in front of the Microchip Mountains.
Draw the mountains.

BONUS! Draw a robot bird in the sky.

The robot family meets a wild bear.
Describe what happens next.

53

Walcott Wolf

Draw your own.

Walcott Wolf needs a trail up the mountain.
Can you draw it?
Add a friend to join him.

Draw a super-huge and heavy backpack on Walcott's back!

BONUS! Give Walcott huge hiking boots.

Make a fancy tent for Walcott
and his daughter Wendy.

Time for bed. Give Walcott and
Wendy warm sleeping bags.

Beatrice Bear

Draw your own.

Beatrice Bear meets her friend.
Draw the friend.

What food is in Beatrice's picnic basket? Draw the foods.

Draw ants all over the bears' food.

·········· | BONUS! | How to Draw Ants ··········

Ivan the Inventor

Draw your own.

BONUS! Put an invention in his hand.

Ivan invented a high-tech kite. Draw it!

Ivan's bubble machine makes bubbles of any shape.
Fill the page with bubbles!

Ivan has a machine that throws disks.
Draw something to catch the disk.

Story Starter

Ivan accidentally gets stuck in one of his bubbles and floats into the sky. Explain what happens next!

Find and Color the Hidden Items

book · sock · tent · glasses · seashell · cupcake · bandage · pencil · flag · ladder

Greta Gator

Draw your own.

Greta Gator is going parasailing. Draw her.

Create a super-cool Jet Ski
for Greta Gator to ride.

BONUS! Draw big splashy waves behind her.

Greta Gator has some silly water skis.
Draw them.

What happens when Greta Gator tries to ski jump over a pyramid of water-skiing ducks? Write a story.

Deegan Dragon blows fire to get the grill cooking. Draw the fire.

BONUS! Add your favorite food to the grill.

75

Deegan needs a chef's hat and
an exciting design for his apron.

Create a super-tall burger for hungry Deegan.

BONUS! What does Deegan like on his burger? Draw it!

Deegan is hungry!
How many hot dogs can you fit in his mouth?

······ **BONUS!** How to Draw Hot Dogs ······

Story Starter

79

Poodle Pearl and Bulldog Benny

Draw your own.

Draw your own.

It's a pool day!
Draw Pearl and Benny
in the pool.

BONUS! Give them pool toys.

Draw floats for Pearl and Benny to relax on.

Pearl is scared of
the loopy water slide.
Can you draw it?

Story Starter

Describe what happens when Edgar the Elephant does a cannonball into the pool.

HINT! Draw a huge splash.

Find and Color the Hidden Items

Draw your own.

Draw your own.

Becky loves riding her scooter.
Draw a friend for her
to scoot with.

Create a super-duper tree house.
Add more rooms and ladders.

BONUS! Draw kids in the treehouse.

Draw another kid jumping on the trampoline.

Draw a hammock for Becky to read in.

Time to get wet!
Draw another kid playing with
Becky in the sprinkler.

BONUS! Draw more water coming out of the sprinkler.

The Super-Duper Summer Parade
starts with loud horns!
Give Roller-Skating Rhino a big horn
and Owen a small horn.

BONUS! Give Tara Turtle a HUGE feathery headpiece.

The pals are holding a big wacky balloon.
Can you draw it?

The drums are booming!
Give Poodle Pearl a large drum.
Give Beatrice Bear
an even bigger drum!

BONUS! Mr. Robot is cheering! Give him pompoms!

Design a summer flag for
Monkey Pirate to wave.
Give Deegan sunglasses.

Did you find all the suns?
Color the page number that corresponds to the sun you found.

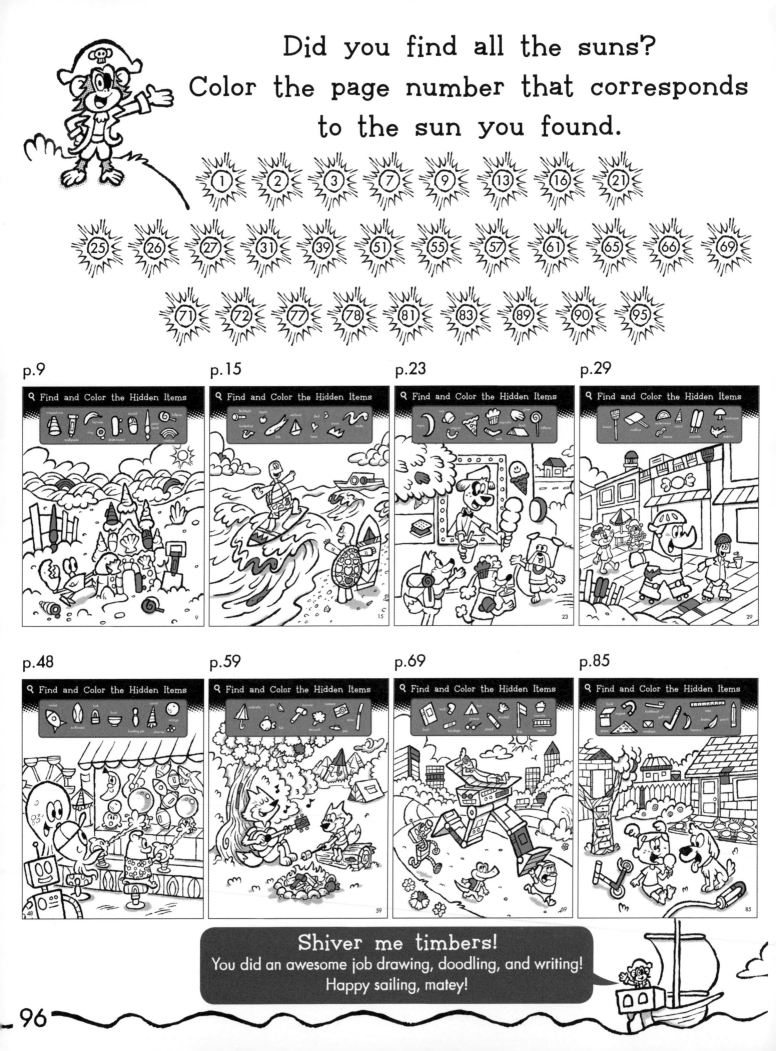

1 2 3 7 9 13 16 21

25 26 27 31 39 51 55 57 61 65 66 69

71 72 77 78 81 83 89 90 95

p.9

p.15

p.23

p.29

p.48

p.59

p.69

p.85

Shiver me timbers!
You did an awesome job drawing, doodling, and writing!
Happy sailing, matey!